Note to parents and teachers

Acted out by a class of schoolchildren, **The Story of Christmas** will help inspire other children to put on their own nativity play. The scenes are presented in a simple but effective way, with colorful costumes, painted backdrops, and household props that provide lots of practical ideas for planning a play, encouraging children to make their own costumes, paint their own scenery, and write their own script. Each episode of the story, presented across a double page, can be used to promote discussion, whether at home or in the classroom. Young children will enjoy this special story of Jesus' birth.

A DK PUBLISHING BOOK

Editor Fiona Campbell
U.S. Editor Camela Decaire
Designers Sarah Scrutton and Sheilagh Noble

Illustrated by Nancy Anderson
Photography by Andy Crawford
Costumes designed by Victoria Patrick

DK would like to give special thanks to the children of class 2 and their teacher, Mary Mullarkey, from John Betts' Primary School, Hammersmith, London

Additional acknowledgments Gillian Allan, Louise Barratt, Rintje Howe, Adrienne Hutchinson, Intellectual Animals, Gary Ombler, Lee Simmons, Jane Yorke. Additional photography by Jane Burton, Gordon Clayton, Mike Dunning

First American Edition, 1995
2 4 6 8 10 9 7 5 3

Published in the United States by
Dorling Kindersley Publishing, Inc., 95 Madison Avenue
New York, New York 10016

Library of Congress Cataloguing-in-Publication Data.

Ganeri, Anita, 1961–
    The story of Christmas / retold by Anita Ganeri – 1st Amer. ed.
       p.   cm.
    ISBN 0-7894-0146-0
    1. Jesus Christ–Nativity–Juvenile literature.
    [1. Jesus Christ–Nativity.]   I. Title
    BT315.2.G35   1995
    232.92–dc20   94-44796
                                                               CIP
                                                               AC

Color reproduction by Dot Gradations, Essex
Printed and bound in Italy by L.E.G.O.

THE STORY OF CHRISTMAS

Retold by Anita Ganeri

"A town in Galilee, named Nazareth"

Long ago in the town of Nazareth, in Galilee, lived a young woman named Mary. She sang as she helped her mother with the daily household chores and chatted with friends when they came to visit.

Mary was engaged to be married to a man named Joseph. He was a good man who worked as a carpenter in Nazareth.

"Fear not, Mary, thou hast found favor with God."

One day, when Mary was busy baking bread, a shining figure suddenly appeared before her.

Alarmed, Mary dropped her bread in fright. But this was the angel Gabriel. He had come to deliver a special message from God.

"Don't be afraid Mary. God has chosen you to be the mother of a baby."

"You shall call him Jesus. He will be a very special king."

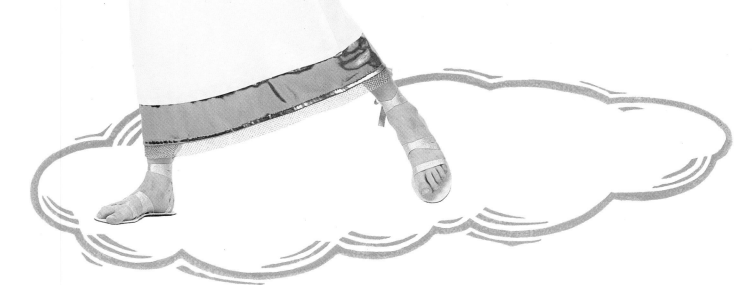

Mary hurried to tell Joseph of the angel's news. Joseph was troubled, wondering if their marriage should go ahead now that Mary was expecting a baby.

But that night, in a dream, an angel told him he should still get married – all would be well.

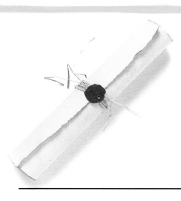

"Unto the city of David, called Bethlehem"

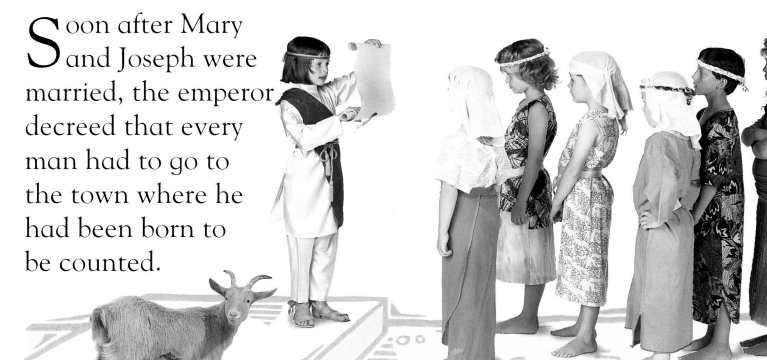

Soon after Mary and Joseph were married, the emperor decreed that every man had to go to the town where he had been born to be counted.

Joseph had been born in Bethlehem, far away. So Mary and Joseph packed up their belongings and set off on the journey.

Days later, they reached Bethlehem, dusty and tired. The town was crowded with people.

"There was no room for them at the inn."

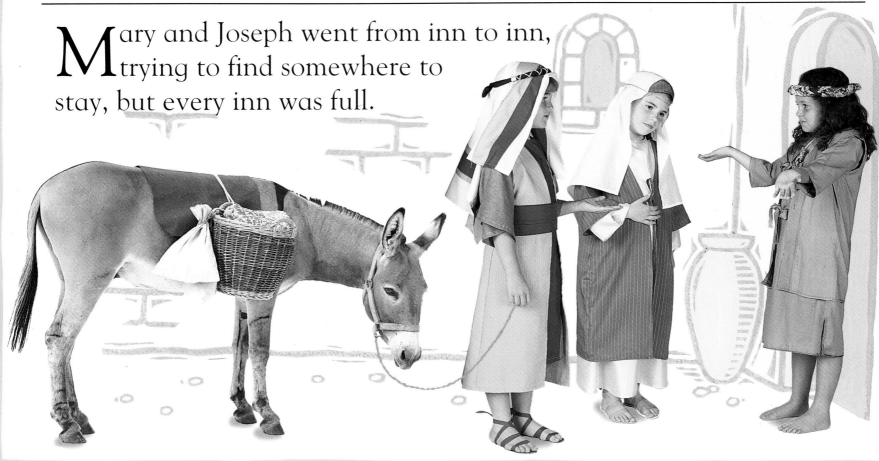

Mary and Joseph went from inn to inn, trying to find somewhere to stay, but every inn was full.

Finally, a kind innkeeper took pity on them. He had no spare rooms, but he did have a stable.

Mary was worried. She knew that her baby could be born at any time now.

Mary peered inside and smiled. She was happy to have found a warm and clean place to rest at last.

"And the time came for the baby to be born."

Later that night, in the snug little stable, Mary's baby, a boy, was born.

She called him Jesus, the name the angel had given her, and wrapped him warmly in a blanket.

Gently, Mary laid
Jesus in a manger
filled with soft hay.

Mary and Joseph
smiled happily at
each other. They knew
Jesus was a very special baby.

Later, Mary rested while
Joseph watched over
her and the baby.
"How peaceful they look,"
he thought tenderly.

"There were shepherds abiding in the fields."

Meanwhile, on a nearby hillside, some shepherds, tending their flock of sheep, had gathered together to tell stories through the night.

16

Suddenly, a brilliant light filled the sky. An angel appeared before the fearful shepherds.

"I bring you good tidings of great joy."

"This day, a baby has been born in Bethlehem. You will find him lying in a manger."

"Glory to God in the highest"

As the shepherds looked up, astonished, the sky blazed with light. Angels appeared, shining brighter than the brightest stars, singing and praising God.

"Peace on Earth."

"Good will to all people."

Then, just as suddenly, the angels were gone. The shepherds were very excited.

"We must go to Bethlehem at once, to see the baby and worship him."

And off they went, taking a tiny lamb with them for a gift.

"They found the baby lying in a manger."

T he shepherds hurried to Bethlehem as fast as they could. There, in the stable, they found Mary, Joseph, and the baby Jesus.

The shepherds knelt quietly by the manger, careful not to wake the sleeping baby. Filled with love, they presented the lamb to the baby before returning to their sheep in the hills.

On the way back, they told everyone they met about the amazing things they had seen and heard.

21

"We have seen his star in the east."

Far away to the east, some wise men saw a bright new star in the sky. The star was a sign that a king had been born.

The wise men followed the star to Jerusalem, in search of the new ruler.

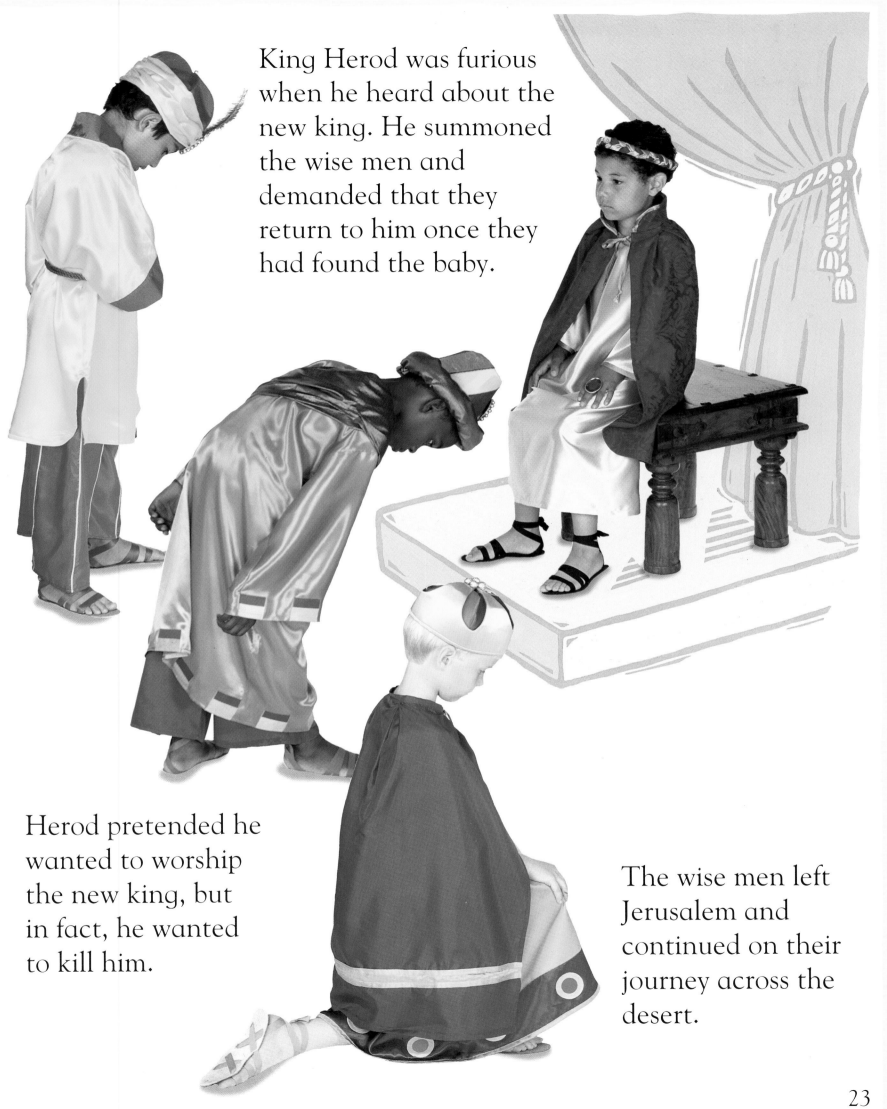

King Herod was furious when he heard about the new king. He summoned the wise men and demanded that they return to him once they had found the baby.

Herod pretended he wanted to worship the new king, but in fact, he wanted to kill him.

The wise men left Jerusalem and continued on their journey across the desert.

"Lo, the star went before them."

It guided them on their way, leading them to the town of Bethlehem.

The wise men rested by day and traveled by night so that they could follow the great star.

24

Once the star reached Bethlehem, it glowed stronger and brighter than before. Finally, it came to rest over the stable where Jesus lay.

They had found the king at last!

"They presented unto him gifts."

The wise men went into the stable carrying gifts for Jesus. They brought caskets of precious gold, sweet-smelling frankincense, and healing myrrh.

The wise men bowed down and worshiped the baby.

Later that night, each was warned in a dream not to return to King Herod. So the men traveled back to their country by a different route.

"Take the child and flee to Egypt."

Soon after, Joseph, too, was warned of King Herod's wicked plan to kill Jesus. An angel told him to flee to Egypt with his family.

Joseph woke Mary. They quietly gathered up their belongings and crept away through the narrow streets of Bethlehem.

Their journey took many days, but they finally reached Egypt safely.

Here they stayed until an angel brought Joseph good news. King Herod had died, making it safe for the family to return home.

Each year, we celebrate the birth of the baby Jesus. We call this special time "Christmas."

29